This adult swear word coloring book
Belongs To

Cock
Sock

EVER
LASTING
CUM
STOPPER

POLE
HOLE

Indiana
Bones
And The
Temple Of
Doom

FUCK
HOLE

VAG

Cold
Cut
Combo

Meat
Locker

Piss
flaps

Dildo
Hotel

HONEY
POT

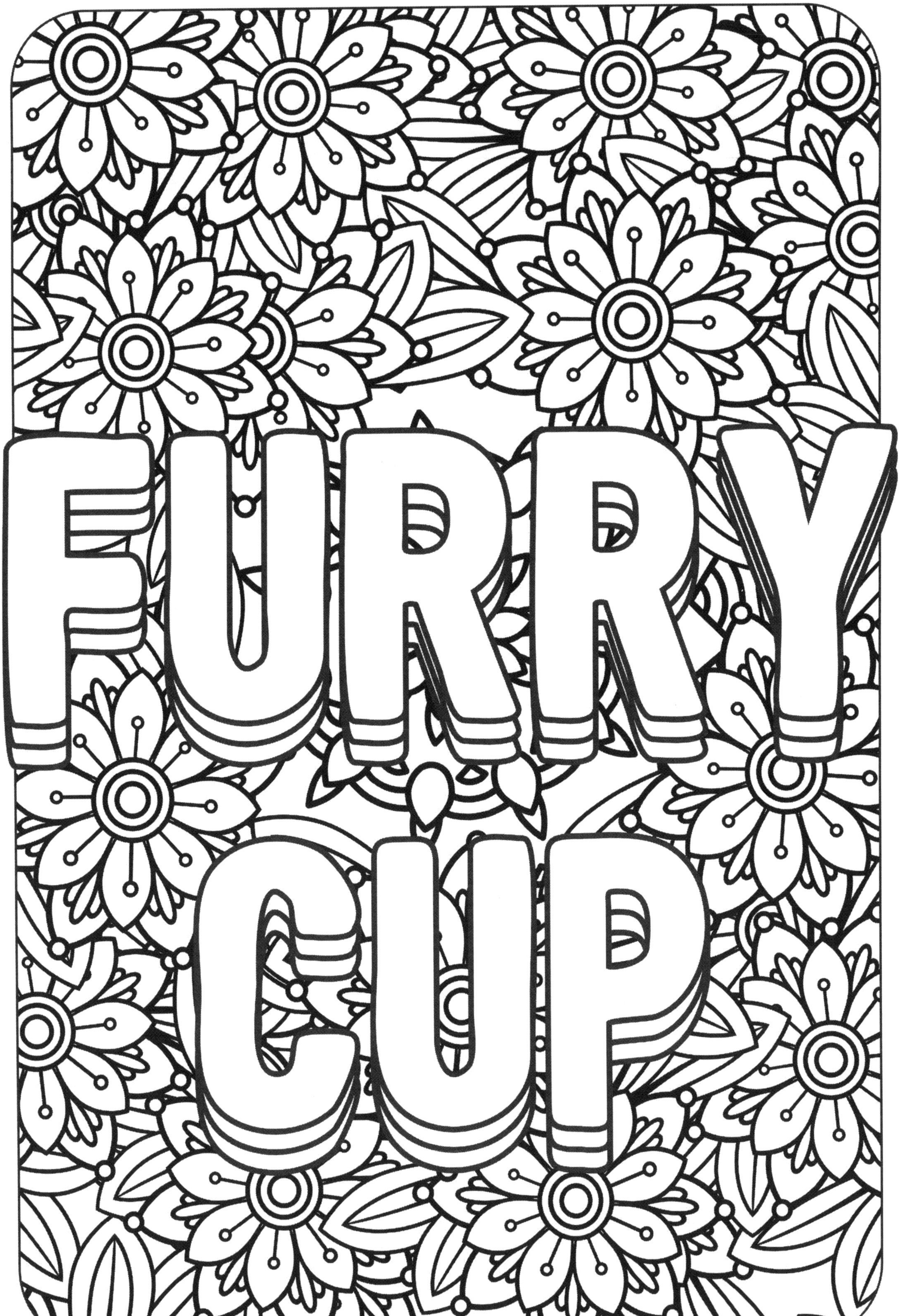
FURRY
CUP

Clit
Slit

POOL
PEPPER

TINY
AXE
WOUND

Furry
Pink
Mink

YOU!

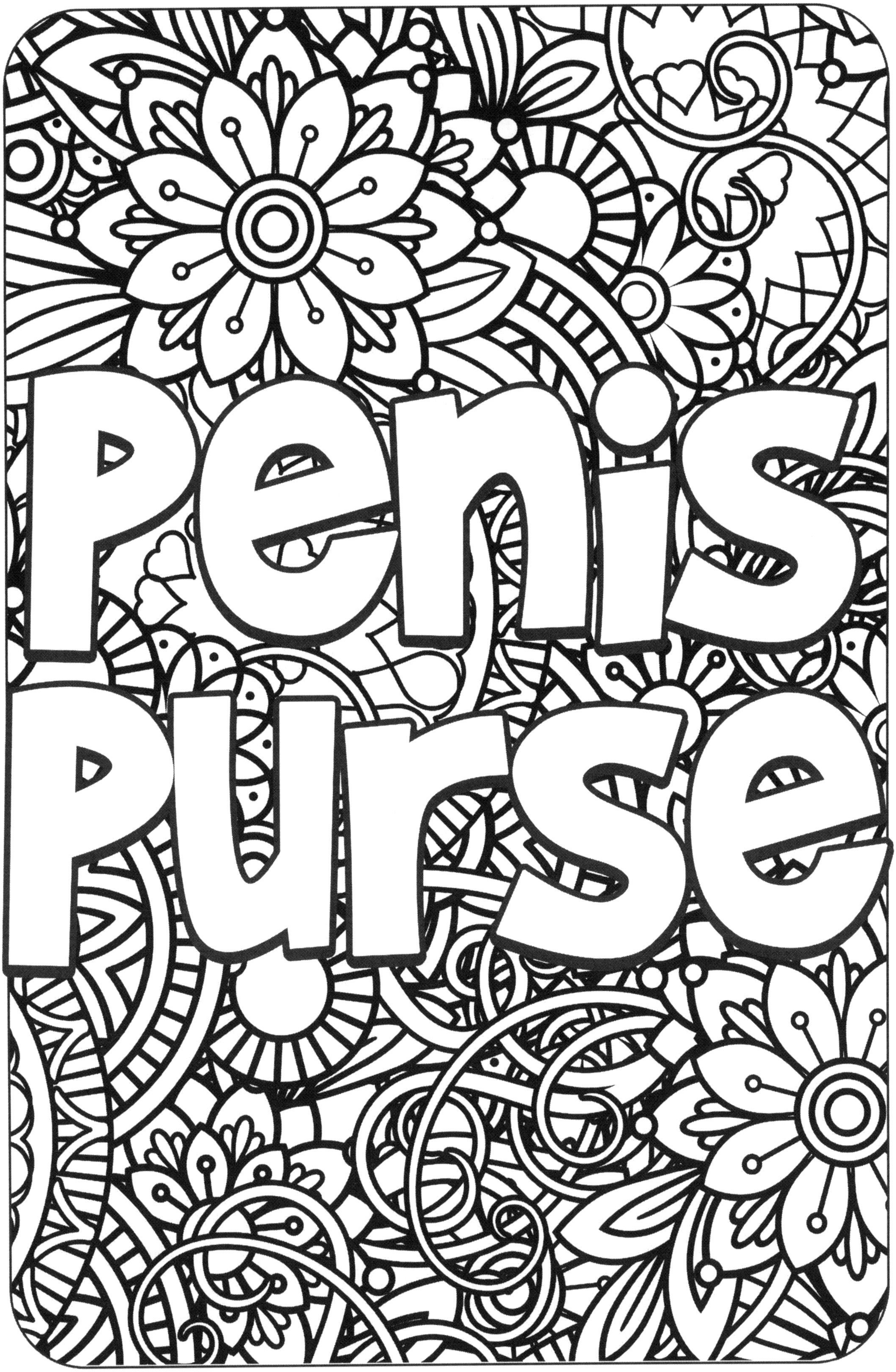
Penis
Purse

Cha
Cha

HAPPY
FLAPPY

Fucking
Color
Testing
Page

Made in the USA
Columbia, SC
18 October 2024

44547675R00026